REALMS AND DIMENSIONS OF THE SUPERNATURAL

REALMS AND DIMENSIONS
OF THE SUPERNATURAL

Janice Fountaine

ISBN: 978-1-58930-242-6
Library of Congress Control Number: 2009912064

This book is dedicated to the Body of Christ.

May you access the knowledge and resources which God has made available to you, within the realms of the supernatural, to fulfill His purpose in you and witness the kingdom of God come, in earth, as it is in heaven.

ACKNOWLEDGEMENTS

I acknowledge God the Father, God the Son and God the Holy Spirit as the one and only sovereign God, to whom there is no competition, for besides Him there is no other.

I thank my husband Elder Darnell Fountaine, my mother Lenora Battle and the members and partners of Kingdom Empowerment Churches of the Apostolic and Prophetic International for their support and encouragement.

CONTENTS

INTRODUCTION

There is so much, about God, that must be downloaded into the spirits of mankind. God desires to impart, to us, through His Spirit, kingdom authority and domination; however, we must come before Him, long enough, to be positioned to receive them.

God says that, "My people do not know me. They have not seen me. They have not heard me. They have not touched me. They have not come into an intimate enough relationship with me, whereas I can reveal the inner me, to them. They have not come into an intimate enough relationship with me, whereas I can reveal the intricacies of My being, to them."

God told me, "I want to show the Body of Christ what I showed to Moses. (Exodus 33:19-34:6). I want to show them the fullness of Myself. I want to show them the very essence of My being. I want to show them My glory. They have not come into my presence, into the depth that I require of them. Therefore, they do not know Me. They do not see Me. They do not hear Me and they have not touched Me."

Body of Christ, we know God by what He reveals to us. This revelation is what gives us the weighty ideas, the supernatural wisdom and the knowledge and the understanding, that we need to fulfill His kingdom purpose, in us. God gives us revelation knowledge, into His inner being, so that we will know how to operate, in the spirit realm, at any given time.

God declares that Christians have not come into His presence, not only to know, but to see the activities and movements of His Spirit in the supernatural and manifested in the natural. He says that they have not seen, enough of Him, to touch and know the intricacies of His being, personality and character. They have not seen, enough of Him, to witness the awe of His glory. They have not seen the essence of Him, which are the activities, works and movements of His Spirit. They have not seen the manifestation of His glory and presence, upon their lives, to the extent that He has ordained, for them.

Because the Body of Christ have not known, seen or touched Him to the extent that they must, they cannot hear the voice of God in the stillness of time, in the fire, in the rain or in the wind of His Spirit or the trumpet of His call. In essence, they are operating as kings without the power thereof.

God wants and requires His Church, the Body of Christ, to be operating to its fullest capacity. This is a must condition for them, so He is shifting the Body, in the realm of the Spirit. He is elevating them into areas and arenas that will allow them to come into the relationship, with Him, that is needed and necessary to obtain kingdom dominion, on earth, for end-time warfare and harvesting.

God is a Spirit and He operates from the realm of the supernatural. We must do so, as well, by His Spirit. We have been pre-destined to do so. We have been designed to operate, in the realms of the supernatural, by the Spirit of God, communicating with our spirit. The Spirit of God is our connection piece to God. He is the vein of our communication between us and God. He is the umbilical cord which has never been cut. He is our channel, to the Revelation Knowledge, which God wants to give, to us, about Himself and His kingdoms, so that we can grasp the height, depth, breath and length, of the kingdom of God and the kingdoms of earth and this world and walk in kingdom authority. The Holy Spirit is God upon us, in us and through us.

The church is being overwhelmed, by the enemy, on too many angles, because they are not taking advantage of the opportunity given, to them, which exists within the supernatural realms and are an integral part of their lives and those around them. The revelation of God will help many to understand the dynamics, of why and how things occurred, in their lives and the world that exists around them.

The Body of Christ must be constantly aware, of the supernatural operating and existing around them. The strategy of the enemy is to have them not aware, by making this reality, appear to be somewhat of an illusion, or too unreal, to be true.

God's shifting, of the Body of Christ, will cause them to be imploded with an outpouring of His Spirit, into positions, where they can receive and apply His outpour, to His end-time purpose, which concerns the things that are, the things that are to come and the things that must be.

This supernatural outpour is being released, upon those who realize, that fellowship and worship, of God, is a privilege with calculated and intentional purpose. It is also being released upon those who will apply His glory, which is the essence of Him, to kingdom purpose; supernaturally impacting communities, nations, regions and worlds, all to the glory of God.

During the shift, of the Body of Christ, there is going to be several movements within the Five-fold ministry offices. There is now, a powerful Apostolic and Prophetic Movement, in which God is equipping, empowering, anointing and sending forth His apostles and prophets, to ignite the shift, with His spoken word.

In the Revelation of Jesus Christ to the Apostle John we read throughout chapter 1, "He that hath an ear let Him hear what the Spirit saith unto the churches." We must incline our spiritual ear, to God, so that we can hear Him. We must hear God, in worship, within the depths of His secret place and we must hear God through the activities and movements of His Spirit within and around us.

Hearing God, through His Prophets and other vessels, is predicated on a prepared ear. This prepared ear can only be built and sustained, off of an intimate worship relationship, with God.

The purpose, of this book, is to:
- make Christians aware of the realms of the supernatural.
- help Christians understand the dynamics and inner workings of the supernatural realms.
- show the importance of the supernatural realms in the lives of mankind.
- heighten one's desire to move in the realms of the supernatural and fulfill God's purpose, for them, in the kingdom.

In reading this book, you will begin to tap into the very essence of God and His purpose in you. It will be up to you; however, to remain in the fellowship, for continuous growth and development in Him. You must, aggressively and progressively press into God, if you are to have any real and measurable impact, for the Kingdom of God, both individually and corporately.

Be blessed and be encouraged, as the Lord takes you into places of the supernatural, which you have never been before and will never want to leave.

THE SUPERNATURAL

"In the beginning God created the heavens and the earth."

Genesis 1:1

The supernatural or realm of the Spirit is a place of being, created and housed by God. It is the seat of and the expanse of the essence and kingdom of God. The supernatural realm does not house God but God houses it. It is within the space of the essence and being of God.

The space of the supernatural is to God, as water is to whatever vessel it is poured into. It takes on the shape of that which it is within. It expands if and to whatever dimensions God chooses to expand Himself. In other words, the scope of the supernatural begins and ends with God, to whom there is only beginning and no end. The end is so intertwined with the beginning that there is never an end. Where the end would be, the beginning is. The scope is, as God is, Alpha and Omega. The beginning and the end is God Himself. The beginning is the end and the end is the beginning.

The world of the supernatural is an active and existent world endlessly superior to the natural world in which we live. Its diameter is limitless, without boundaries, eternal and everlasting.

For many, to believe in a world outside of earth, is a challenge, because they are accustomed to seeing in the natural rather than the supernatural. As a result, the existence of the supernatural world has seemingly been somewhat of a myth or a passing thought, based on traditional belief, to many in the Body of Christ, rather than a reality. In other words, many believe but they don't believe. Tradition says believe, so they exercise surface belief. A belief that is all too often predicated on what one sees, with the physical eye, rather than what one knows, with the spiritual eye, through the exercising of his faith in and experience with God.

Many believe God, without tapping into the essence of God and the world in which He lives. They are accustomed, to operating their lives, according to the physical series of events and conditions that occur within their lives and the lives of those around them. Consequently, many have not come to know God, in the depths of His being, which is the world of the supernatural. This is the world where the seat of God's domain is.

What so many people are not cognizant of is that mankind is nonexistent outside of the supernatural realm of the spirit. This is why God put a spirit in mankind. 1 Thessolonians 5:23 is read, "Now may the God of peace Himself sanctify you completely; and may your whole spirit, soul and body be preserved blameless at the coming of our Lord Jesus Christ." John 4:24 is read, "God is Spirit, and those who worship Him, must worship in spirit and truth." We must be in consistent fellowship and communication with God, thus interacting, within the supernatural realm, in which He exists.

This is the world where the Body of Christ must become progressively interactive, so that we can live life abundantly and fulfill God's purpose in us.

REALMS OF THE SUPERNATURAL

"For even if I should boast somewhat more about our authority, which the Lord gave us for edification and not for your destruction, I shall not be ashamed…"

2 Corinthians 10:8

The scope of the supernatural is made up of realms. It is a must and of utmost urgency and importance that the people of God come into the knowledge of these realms, to walk in kingdom authority, in earth as it is done in heaven.

Realms are areas or arenas of divine authority within the scope of God Himself. They are domains, areas, arenas or zones of territory, within the supernatural, that a Christian has been predestined, by God, to move and operate in, with kingship anointing, authority and domination.

Every Christian moves and operates in divers realms, throughout their lives, relative to their purpose in the kingdom.

The realms of the supernatural is not a spooky place, as the enemy would have mankind to believe, but it is God's dominion and resource center for the Body of Christ.

Within it is all that God has for mankind. It is therefore; a conduit for the Body of Christ. Resources, within the supernatural, are made available to an individual according to the predetermined and distributed allotment, afforded to him, by God.

According to Jeremiah 1:5 and Zechariah 2:1-6, this allotment has been pre-determined by God, based on His foreknowledge of the individual and His divine purpose for him.

God created and resides within the scope of Himself. This scope is endless and unlimited. This scope is called the realm of God. Within the realm of God are subordinate realms of the supernatural. These subordinate realms are areas of activity, interest and authority of which someone is dominant.

Within the subordinate realms of the supernatural, God has made available, kingdom resources necessary for man to dominate earth and live an abundant life. Kingdoms, such as earth, or as it is sometimes referred to as the kingdom of man, are dominated and operated within the resources, boundaries and limitations of the particular realm.

These realms are accessed by mankind, according to the pre-destined and pre-determined authority, given to them, by God. 2 Corinthians 10:8, Jeremiah 1:12.

God's is sovereign and His realm or arena is unlimited. It expands as far as God Himself does or chooses for it to. It encompasses the essence and being of God and the essence and being of God dictates its scope.

The realms in which mankind are given authority, are accessed within the boundaries and limitations, given to him, by God, to fulfill His purpose in them.

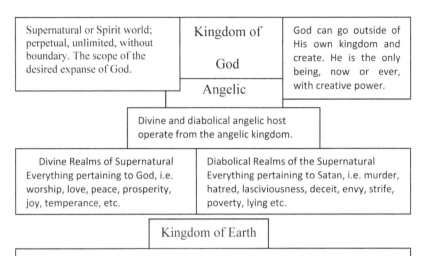

Supernatural or Spirit world; perpetual, unlimited, without boundary. The scope of the desired expanse of God.	Kingdom of God	God can go outside of His own kingdom and create. He is the only being, now or ever, with creative power.

Angelic

Divine and diabolical angelic host operate from the angelic kingdom.

Divine Realms of Supernatural Everything pertaining to God, i.e. worship, love, peace, prosperity, joy, temperance, etc.	Diabolical Realms of the Supernatural Everything pertaining to Satan, i.e. murder, hatred, lasciviousness, deceit, envy, strife, poverty, lying etc.

Kingdom of Earth

An extension of the kingdom of God. Mankind is predestined to rule over, in addition to other kingdoms of this world, (animal, plant, water, atomic etc.) through domination in and over divine and diabolical realms of the supernatural. The kingdom of God is wherever God is. This is why His kingdom is in earth, because He is on earth, because of the meritorious acts of Jesus Christ, and through the indwelling of man by His Spirit.

Within the realm of God Himself, which is the scope of the essence of God, is the kingdom of God and all other kingdoms, as well as, other realms. God Himself exists outside of His own kingdom. Genesis 1:1 is read, "In the beginning, God...." In other words, in the beginning. There in the beginning, is God. There is no area or space that can encompass God, His knowledge, His presence or His authority. God exists beyond the scope of Himself because there is neither an end nor a limit to His existence and creative power. God has the power to create an extension of Himself by Himself. In addition, He is the supreme authority of all things existent; past, present and future. There is none other, as, or besides Him. There never has been or ever will be. Therefore, because Jesus Christ brought mankind back in fellowship with God, there is within the realms of the supernatural, everything mankind needs to dominate earth and live a victorious, abundant and everlasting life.

There are many people in the Body of Christ who are trying to root out, pull down, throw down, destroy, build and plant without tapping into the resources, which are available in the supernatural, to acquire these things. As a result, they witness unanswered prayers, ill-effectiveness in ministering and deliverance and an overall defeated life. They move about with the assumption of power without being effectively empowered. Many yokes are remaining unbroken, the dead are not living again and the dry bones are still dry. The sick are getting sicker and the unsaved are still waiting, moaning and groaning, for a more visible God and a better life.

The Body of Christ, as a whole, is not walking in kingdom authority. They are in a weak and vulnerable condition because they are not actively engaged, in the world of the supernatural, as they should be. Many have done well in having church, but now they must be the church that God ordained and Jesus Christ is coming back for. In other words, many Christians are having more church than they are being the church.

The church is to be a power tool. Through the five-fold ascensions gifts, that Jesus Christ left to the church, according to Ephesians 4:11, the Body of Christ is to be the extension of the love, power and authority of Jesus Christ here on earth.

The church is a body, of baptized believers, with each individual having a spirit that is housed in their body. The Spirit always supersedes the natural. So we are spirit-man, with our spirit, supposedly, being the dominate force within us.

We are Spirit beings housed in a natural body. The kingdom of God is at hand and we, His extension, must be in the place, the position, and the condition for eternal and everlasting life.

To insure that the enemy is defeated on all accounts, the Body of Christ must be holy, empowered and operating in the authoritative realms of the supernatural. The lost souls or lost citizens, of the kingdom of God, as well as, predestined kings of God's extended kingdom, earth, must be brought to Christ.

Now, in this prophetic movement of time, in order for the Body of Christ, to move in the fullness of their divine nature, there must be a transition of their thought patterns. There must be a transition that will result in their thinking, living and operating, within the realms of the supernatural; powerfully, boldly and confidently.

This transition must come mainly, because there has been a lack, of many, in church leadership, to nourish the sheepfold, in the reality and practice of believing and operating in the power and authority made available to the Body of Christ, through the realms of the supernatural.

God has found the Body to be weak, frail and powerless. As a result there are movements taking place, in the realm of the supernatural, orchestrated by God, which are causing a paradigm shift in the Body of Christ. This shift will make the existence of the supernatural a reality for Christians and usher them into their proper positions of domination for kingdom authority and harvesting in these end-times.

The activation, of this paradigm shift, will come by way of the mouths of the prophetic. The facilitation and maintenance of the Body will come through the apostolic and other gifts of the five-fold and will trickle down to the pew being empowered and motivated as well. This is why those who move in the office and other ministries of the five-fold must be righteous, pure, holy, unified, prepared, anointed and appointed.

There will be a visible change in Christians' thinking and there will be a visible change in their outlook concerning the supernatural. The transition is taking place by divine movements, in the supernatural realm, which are causing a shift in the Body of Christ. These movements in the supernatural are being manifested through the Apostolic and Prophetic Movements on earth. The word which God is raising and sending prophets forth, to speak, is a word of preparation, activation and warning, to the Body of Christ. He is shifting them into alignment, with His will, concerning them and their thoughts and attitude regarding the supernatural and their walking in kingdom authority.

In addition, God is bringing the apostles into position, so that they will lay the foundation and maintain order, for the next move, within the Body of Christ, once the shift has taken place.

The realm of the supernatural must be seen by us as a lifestyle, a way of living, a way of moving about, in our daily walk, with God. It is not a complex phenomenon, but rather a comprehendible and essential one, for those who are willing to understand, the true meaning of divinity and the process of kingdom authority, as well as, learn of and become actively involved in its movements and activities, as led by the Spirit of God.

Understanding the supernatural is beyond the vein of natural reasoning, therefore cannot be understood without revelation from the Spirit of God.

The realms of the supernatural are spirit domains, which are real and necessary places for the Body of Christ to operate in, through their spirit, so that they may walk in the kingdom authority that God has ordained for them. Mankind sees in realms what he cannot see in the natural.

Mankind was given a spirit so that he could communicate with God to operate and dominate in the spirit or supernatural realms.

Mankind must have supernatural resources to rule earth and other kingdoms of the world that he has been given dominion over. These supernatural resources are housed and available in divers and numerous areas, for mankind to obtain, for his use in kingdom authority and domination.

Christians are to move and operate in realms under the unction and guidance of the Spirit of God. The Spirit of God enables them to always be mindful, of the will and movements, within the divine and diabolical realms of the supernatural, with an ear to the pulse of God, so that one may ensure that they say and do according to the will of God at any given time and in any given situation or setting.

A person cannot be part spirit and not be tapped into the realm of the Spirit. In other words, one must be tapped into and identify with every part of himself. A person must know who he (mankind) is. He is a spirit housed in a body. Therefore he must walk by the Spirit of God. When Jesus Christ returns, everyone will be changed from mortality to immortality. They will change from part spirit to all spirit. Christians will be unlimited in scope, unto God.

There are natural and supernatural realms and there are divine and diabolical realms. The only way to dominate in any kingdom is to have access and authority to realms relating to the kingdom. The divine realms are in particular areas such as: healing, prosperity, worship, knowledge, wisdom, leadership, etc. and begin at graduating dimensions or levels of authority. A person moves within a realm based on divine release of revelation knowledge and one's ability and success in maturing and applying that knowledge, to their responsibilities and assignments, relative to their purpose in that particular realm.

The predestined and pre-determined realms, for an individual, have been ordained and orchestrated by God before they were in their mother's womb (see Jeremiah 1:5). In addition, God is the only one who knows when and what it takes to get to various realms and dimensions within those realms. An individual may reach their peak in a realm, at any point, while another person operating or exercising authority, in that same realm, may excel over the first person. This elevation is pre-determined by God, again depending upon one's assignment in that realm. One individual may excel in revelation knowledge and have witnessed, a greater extent of manifestation, than another, who operates in the same realm, because his assignment, in that particular realm, is varied and perhaps more in depth.

HEART OF A REALM

(As seen, in an open vision, from God)

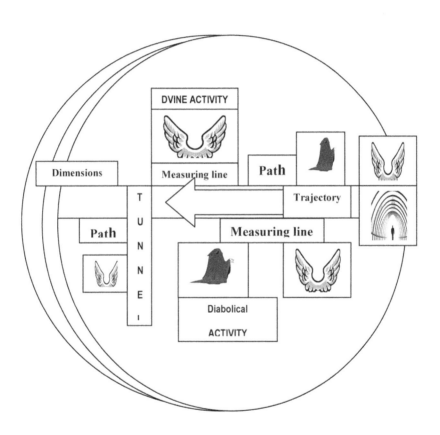

TERRITORY

"For we dare not class ourselves or compare ourselves with those who commend themselves. But,
they measuring themselves by themselves, and
comparing themselves among themselves, are not
wise. We, however, will not boast beyond measure,
but within the limits of the sphere which God
appointed us-a sphere which especially includes
you. For we are not overextending ourselves (as
if our authority did not extend to you), for it was
to you that we came with the gospel of Christ; not
boasting of things beyond measure, that is, in other
men's labor, but having hope, that as your faith is
increased, we shall be greatly enlarged by you in our
sphere, to preach the gospel in the regions beyond
you, and not to boast in another man's sphere of
accomplishment."

2 Corinthians 10:12-16

Territory, in the realms of the supernatural, is the extent of
space or authority, within a realm, that one is given, whereas he
can access resources necessary to fulfill God's purpose in him.

One of the most defining attributes of a king is his territory.
The extent of a king's territory, within a kingdom, helps define
His wealth and is an indication or measuring point, along with
its citizenry, as to the strength and vulnerability of the king and
his kingdom, in relation to his ability to secure and protect the
kingdom in which he dominates, as well as, the probability of
His being able to be dethroned from his kingdom.

What separates God and His kingdom, from any other king or kingdoms, is His territory and citizens. God is the Creator and possessor of all things and without Him nothing was, is or ever will be created.

Earth is an extension of God's kingdom. It is His. "The earth is the Lord's, and all its fullness, The world and those who dwell therein." Psalms 24:1

God is supreme ruler over the heavens and the earth. He cannot be dethroned, as Lucifer and a host of angels, found out. His territory cannot be taken from Him because He is sovereign and He is the only being ever, or ever to be, with creative power. "To you it was shown, that you might know that the Lord Himself is God; there is none other besides Him. Deuteronomy 4:35.

In extending His kingdom in earth, through man, God included the allotment and transference of territory. This allotment has been spoken, created and obtained in the spirit realm and manifested in the natural, to His citizens, mankind. In order for mankind to operate and walk, in the territory that God has given him to rule over, he must be able to enter the kingdom of God which is in the realm of the supernatural. He must possess certain tools to access the resources needed to fulfill the mandates and assignments that God has given him.

In order for man to access and dominate in the territory and then have the results manifested, on earth, he must have in his possession, the keys to the kingdom of God, given to him for access.

Each of these keys is biblically based attributes, which one must have, to enter the kingdom realm of God, where authority and resources are originated.

- **Salvation** – Salvation is a gift from God. "For by grace you have been saved through faith, and that not of yourselves; it is the gift of God, not of works, lest anyone should boast."

Ephesians 2:8. Unless a man accepts Jesus Christ, as the only begotten, Son of God and believes that God raised Him, from the dead, he cannot enter the kingdom of God. John 14:6 records, "Jesus said to him, "I am the way, the truth and the life. No one comes to the Father except through Me." A person cannot have access to divine territory or authority, for kingdom domination, unless he is saved. If a person is not moving in the divine realms, of the supernatural, then he is operating in the diabolical realms of the supernatural.

- **Faith** – To everyone is given a measure of faith according to their work in God. "For without faith it is impossible to please God. Hebrews 11:6

- **Authority** – Permission to enter realms of the supernatural and pull down, throw down, build, plant, bind, loose and exercise the use of gifts on behalf of the giver. God set Jeremiah over kingdoms and nations with the authority to access the resources, in the spirit realm, needed to fulfill his assignment concerning Israel. "See I have this day set you over nations....... Jeremiah 1:10-12.

As I said before, every Christian has authority, in various realms of the supernatural. God has set His people over kingdoms, nations, regions, cities, states and areas as guards, watchman, captains, princes and kings. These locations and rankings are in the sphere of the spirit realm and are manifested, in the natural realm, on earth.

Throughout the bible men and women exercised authority over kingdoms and dominated in realms of the supernatural—to name a few—Daniel, book of Daniel; Joseph, Genesis 39-41; Huldah, 2 Kings 22:15-17; Jeremiah, book of Jeremiah; Esther, book of Esther; and David, precisely 1st and 2nd Samuel. Their domination manifested in the natural realm but their au- thority refers to a pre-conditioned supernatural domination over those areas with each person having a mandate and assignments, relative to those locations, in the spirit realm and manifested in the natural.

Moving and operating, in authority, produces the manifestation of the presence of God, the glory of God and the Winds of the Spirit of God, in and upon the lives of people.

Because a person possesses these keys he can access territory, in the realms of the supernatural and dominate and rule according to his sphere and measure of authority and He will fulfill God's mandates, assignments and purpose in him. Pulling down, rooting out, destroying, tearing down, building, planting, binding and loosing etc. are results of having keys or access to the kingdom of God and the realms of the supernatural.

- **Knowledge from God** ....Flesh and blood has not revealed this to you, but My Father who is in heaven. Matthew: 16:17

In revelation knowledge, God reveals His feelings, dispositions, plans, instructions, intentions, the position and the condition of the Body of Christ. He exposes diabolical activities, weapons, tools, movements, plans, etc. He reveals the intricacies of the fullness of Himself; which is His personality and His character. The word revelation means to open, reveal or unveil. It gives us the weighty ideas, causes us to understand, gives direction and provides the truth and insight necessary to facilitate mandates, assignments, oppose the enemy, war in diabolical realms etc. necessary to be victorious, reap the harvest and fulfill God's kingdom purpose in us.

There are depths, of worship, in which one is able to partake of God's revelation for his life. A person will never access the resources, needed to fulfill God's purpose, unless he has the revelation, as to how to go about, facilitating God's mandates and assignments. The specifics, of the how to, lies in the mind of the Spirit and must be accessed, in the worship chambers, of God's presence.

BOUNDARIES

"We, however, will not boast beyond measure, but within the limits of the sphere which God appointed us-a sphere which especially includes you."

2 Corinthians 10:13

All territory, within a realm or arena of authority, has boundaries. Boundaries indicate the extent of territory or authority, a person has been given, within a realm. They signify the pre-determined degree and limits, such as, height, depth, length and width of a person's authority relative to God's mandates, assignments and overall purpose, for them, in the kingdom. In 2 Corinthians 10:13, Paul described these boundaries as the sphere of territory in which one ministers. As individuals strive to fulfill God's purposes in them, they must remember that their steps have been established. We exercised our tight, to freewill, in relations to working for the kingdom when we became saved and petitioned God to use us, as He pleases, in our Christian walk.

MEASURING LINE

"Then I raised my eyes and looked, and behold, a man with a measuring line in his hand. So I said, "Where are you going?" And he said to me, "To measure Jerusalem, to see what is its width and what is its length." And there was the angel who talked with me, going out; and another angel was coming out to meet him, who said to him, "Run, speak to this young man, saying: Jerusalem shall be inhabited as towns without walls, because of the multitude of men and livestock in it. For I says the Lord, will be a wall of fire all around her, and I will be the glory in her midst."

                                                                Zechariah 2:1-5

Measuring lines are supernatural markers, used in the realms of the supernatural, by angelic host to mark an individual's territory, in the realm of the supernatural, as instructed by God. A measuring line summarizes the boundaries or limits within a realm in which an individual is allowed to move and operate. These lines make known the length, width, depth and height of a person's allotted territory within a realm. The location of the measuring lines are pre-determined by God based on an individual's assignments, mandates, mantle and overall purpose in the kingdom and can only be seen with a spiritual eye.

These markers were placed based on God's foreknowledge of the individual and his pre-determined mandates, assignments and overall purpose. Jeremiah 1:5.

In the realm of the Spirit, before we were physically in our mother's womb, we were spiritually in our mother's womb in the mind of or realm of the foreknowledge of God. God foreknew us and He sanctified and ordained us unto His kingdom purpose. God saw the choices (acts of our freewill) that our parents made and foreknew the womb of our mothers. It should be accentuated that God pre-determined our assignments and overall purpose, in Him, based on His foreknowledge, of our decision to choose Him, at some point and time in our lives. While we were in our foreknown mother's womb, we were sanctified, given territory and ordained. What an awesome God we serve.

Measuring lines cannot be repented of, just as the gifts cannot. They are based on our pre-determined territory. They were based on God's foreknowledge of us. This is why we should not kick against the pricks, because we will fulfill our purpose in God. A Christian's purpose has already been established. God will break and correct us until we come into the mature place, in Him, that we must be, to fulfill His will in the kingdom.

Our places of indecision are mute and for naught. So, we may as well, just give God, what He wants.

Our territory cannot be enlarged or made smaller. It is pre-measured and pre-marked already, in the realms of the supernatural. It was given to us, before the annals of time, when God took counsel with Himself and foreknew us.

The enlargement of territory, refers to our supernatural ability, to see the expanse of territory, that exists in the realm of the supernatural, which God has given, to us, and is seen more of at various seasons of spiritual elevation. What is given is given. It is already there. The breadth, the length, the width, the height and the depth of our authority is already established. Christians just need to see it. And they will as they mature in God. God does not show it to us all at one time. Our spiritual eyes must become more developed and acute to see further into the realms and dimensions of the supernatural, which is where our territory actually is. The more Christians grow, develop and mature in Christ, the more predestined territory they will see. The more they see, the more they are held accountable to God. "For everyone to whom much is given, from him much will be required;.......Luke 12:48

DIMENSIONS

"That I may know Him and the power of His resurrection, and the fellowship of His sufferings, being
conformed to His death, if by any means, I may
attain to the resurrection from the dead."

Phillipians 3:10

Every realm of the supernatural has depths or stages of
growth, within it, called dimensions. A dimension is any measurable extent or depth within a realm.

The depth, levels or stages, within any given realm that one
operates or moves in, where Revelation Knowledge is imparted
by, the Spirit of God and signifies the degree of authority one is
given, in that realm, are called Dimensions. They determine or
represent the extent of the availability of territorial knowledge
in the realm that one is operating in. The extent to which one
operates in a realm is characterized or measured or indicated by
the demonstration of revelation knowledge and maturity that a
person demonstrates in their daily experience and walk in God
in the assignments.

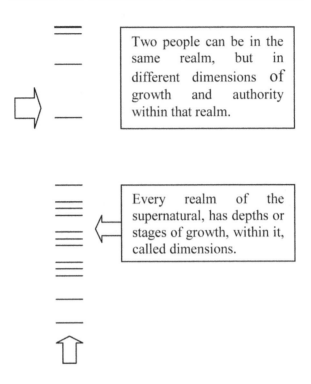

The depth or the dimensions, within a realm, indicates the magnitude of authority one can exert within it. This magnitude of authority signals an individual's ranking, growth and position within a realm. The determining factor pertaining to a person's stage of development or ability to exert authority, within a realm, is the rate of impartation of revelation knowledge, which one is given about the realm. This revelation knowledge has been pre-determined and extended to a person, by God, based on the individual's mandate, mission and assignments relative to the realm and God's overall purpose, in Him, concerning the kingdom.

A person can have authority and dominate in various realms simultaneously. This person can operate, in more than one realm, at a time and concurrently move in different dimensions or depths, of revelation knowledge, within these various realms.

There are realms of worship, prosperity, healing, deliverance etc. A person may have authority in a realm without current manifestation, of that authority, in the realm. For example, a person may be in a realm, of financial prosperity, yet there is no manifestation of prosperity. At the same time, another person may be in the same realm, yet there is the manifestation of financial prosperity. Both are in the same realm, but are in different dimensions of growth and authority within that realm. The one without manifestation may be in a dimension of preparedness. They may be in the process of receiving revelation knowledge at a level of learning about the divine dynamics and principles or characteristics of prosperity and how to operate using them. He may also be learning about how to identify divine and diabolical activity and the movements associated, with those activities, in that dimension of the realm. The other person may be about to enter another dimension, in that realm, or just seasonably operating in the realm. He has already received revelation, in the dimensions, which the other person is experiencing. He may be operating, in the dimension, whereas he has learned how to invest and diversify. He has received and is being held accountable for receiving and handling more revelation knowledge, as well as, levels of demonic activity and diabolical movements in the realm.

With every different realm, that a person is given authority, there is a season of learning, preparedness, growth, maturity, development and activation, which are characterized by dimensions. Seasons refer to periods of growth and development, as well as, the timing allotted to assignments that a person is given, periodically throughout his life, which culminate God's over-all kingdom purpose in him.

Periods of activation and manifestation are also characterized or measured in dimensions within a certain realm. Some people start at different intervals and some start at the same time, yet there is a quicker demonstration, of manifestation, for some than for others. Dimensional growth within a realm is characterized as elevation. This elevation has been pre-determined based on one's availability, to God, to mature in that season. People are different and it takes more or less for some, to submit to the will of God, than others. Life's position, experiences and encounters can cause acceleration or they can depress the rate of an individual's spiritual growth and development. An individual can neither advance in authority nor have continuous impact, in the kingdom, unless he is elevated in dimensions within a realm.

Dimensions signify growth and authority within a realm. Every person is born with the ability and pre-determined authority to operate within the realms of the supernatural. For a Christian, however, it must be viewed from a kingdom perspective. This ability is characterized by talents that God has placed in each of us, according to His divine purpose. Everyone excels in something. For a person who has accepted Jesus Christ, as his Lord and Savior, this talent will become laced and pack- aged with God's authority and anointing, as signified by his mantle (supernatural covering), as he is elevated into dimen- sions within various realms.

Dimensions are the difference between a person with just a pretty voice (talent without power) and a person with a pretty voice, who ministers to, edifies and breaks yokes of those under the sound of their voice (talent with power).

TRAJECTORIES

> "Indeed, before the day was, I am He; And there
> is no one who can deliver out of My hand; I work
> and who will reverse it?" "This people I have
> formed for Myself; They shall declare My praise."
> Isaiah 43:13, 21

Trajectories are the planned direction, curvature, way or path, within a realm, that has been pre-determined, by God, for an individual to move in. Various individual's paths may or may not subsequently cross with a realm.

There are many different paths in a subordinate supernatural realm and numerous ways or trajectories, which one can move within the realm. The trajectory, of every Christian's path, is pre-determined, by God, based on His foreknowledge and will, concerning the individual, in relation to His kingdom purpose. (Jeremiah 1:5) As a Christian travels, in accordance to trajectories, diabolical movements, created by diabolical activity, are mounted against him. These movements are nullified, broken down, torn down, pulled down, thrown down, defeated, destroyed and disallowed, by the individual. Success depends upon one's ability to use and apply the word of God, one's ability to access supernatural resources and one's ability to operate in the anoint-ing, made available to that individual, for warfare, kingdom domination and authority in supernatural realms.

Also present, along an individual's trajectory or path are divine movements that God orchestrated and ordained, unto you, before you were in your mother's womb. These movements are activated by the divine activity of angels and the Spirit of God or the Holy Spirit, based on worship, prayers, proclamation, speaking the word, and the pre-destined prophetic timing of events and seasons in your life, as well as, other movements relative to the Body of Christ as a whole.

A person's trajectory was based on the application of his free will and choices in life concerning his salvation and his willingness to submit to a supernatural being other than God. Whatever the case, it was foreknown by God. Therefore, a Christian's trajectory is pre-determined by God based on His foreknowledge of the exercising of their freewill to receive Jesus Christ. In other words, if a person accepts the gift of salvation and Jesus Christ as Lord and Saviour, then God determines your trajectory. If a person rejects the gift of salvation and Jesus Christ, as his Lord and Saviour, then he has given Satan control over his life and denied himself a divine trajectory.

An example of a trajectory is the projectile of a rock or a ball which is thrown.

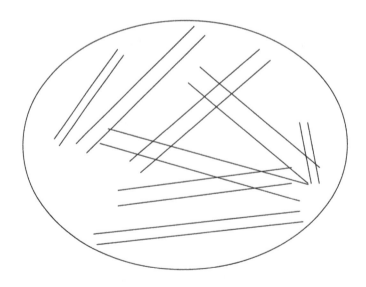

TUNNEL

"Blessing I will bless you, and multiplying I will multiply your descendents as the stars of the heaven and as the sand which is in the seashore; your descendents shall possess the gate of their enemies. In your seed all the nations of the earth shall be blessed, because you have obeyed My voice."

Genesis 22:17-18

A tunnel is an underground passageway. It is the depth of a trajectory. It is endless and unknown to the individual, therefore it is indicated by an end point within a realm, for a particular individual, signaling the height of a dimension of the realm for a person by supernatural measuring or boundary lines or end points.

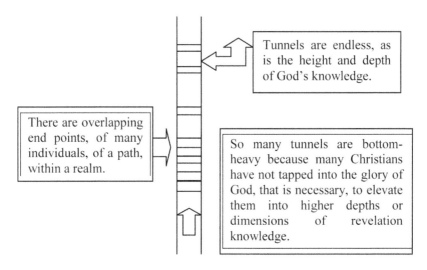

Tunnels are endless, as is the height and depth of God's knowledge.

There are overlapping end points, of many individuals, of a path, within a realm.

So many tunnels are bottom-heavy because many Christians have not tapped into the glory of God, that is necessary, to elevate them into higher depths or dimensions of revelation knowledge.

There is a start point on a path for every Christian, but the point is only known by God. For example, some people Pastor Churches that they have inherited from their parents or which they succeeded another pastor that is established, prosperous and stable. These people must come in on certain growth levels of authority, within certain realms of leadership, etc. to even begin to handle the responsibility that they inherited. Although they may lack in several areas of spiritual maturity, they will need to be moving in areas that may not yet be required of a pastor in a startup or smaller church, as of yet.

The depth of a tunnel determines the extent of a dimension within a realm for an individual. When a person reaches the tunnel on a path in a realm, the extent of revelation knowledge or the dimension has come to an end for that individual. Another person can operate in the same type of realm with more or less depth of revelation knowledge or dimension. For example, two people can move in an apostolic realm with one exceeding or not exceeding the other depending upon their purpose or pre-determined assignment in that realm. One may move in the Office of an Apostle, while the other moves in the Office of a Pastor with an apostolic anointing.

When a person comes out of a tunnel or has reached the breadth or dimension of revelation knowledge, in a particular realm, a person would have reached his pre-determined height of learning and excelling in that realm.

Once a person enters and accesses a realm, he will always have access and authority to that realm. This access and authority is available to him even if he does not utilize the resources allotted, for various reasons, such as his disobedience, sin, lack of faith or lack of self-confidence, slothfulness, etc.

At this point, one would assume that this individual has mastered or reached a maturity level acceptable to God for him to exercise authority in another realm of superior access author-ity, responsibility and accountability.

When there is no new or unchartered realm for a particular individual to move, then he would have reached his peak and prayerfully completed his life's kingdom purpose.

ATMOSPHERIC MOVEMENTS

"Then he said to me, "Do not fear, Daniel, for from the first day that you set your heart to understand, and to humble yourself before your God, your words were heard; and I have come because of your words. But the prince of the kingdom of Persia withstood me twenty-one days; and behold, Michael, one of the chief princes, came to help me......."

Daniel 10:12-13b

Atmospheric movements are events, occurrences and changes, in the atmosphere, of the supernatural and manifested in the natural that affect the position or condition of an individual or group of people.

Movements in the supernatural are based on or facilitated by the Holy Spirit and divine or diabolical angelic activity. Angelic activity brings into being, that which has been commanded by God, spoken by man or gained access to by the enemy.

The activity and movements that affect the atmosphere are spiritually discerned. Everyone has a naturally embedded ability to discern right from wrong. Another level of discernment comes from the impartation, of the gift of discernment, by the Holy Spirit of God. There are dimensions of discernment that are activated in the authoritative realms of the supernatural. These dimensions of discernment allows one to sense and determine past, present and future divine or diabolical activity and movements in the atmosphere and their effects. Demonic angels or hosts do not leave; they lie in wait and watch over their activity and movements as a crouching tiger. God told Cain in Genesis

4:7; "If thou doest well, shalt thou not be accepted? And if thou doest not well, sin lieth at the door. And unto thee shall be his desire, and thou shalt rule over him."

Unholy words spoken in the atmosphere, freely, by a person with the intention of fulfilling his various agendas, in actuality, release diabolical activity in support of the devil's agenda to steal, kill and to destroy (1 John 10:10). The enemy legally aligns himself and his works, with a person, through the ungodly words that the person speaks and the ungodly thoughts which he entertains.

The devil then uses worldly systems, to aid him, in facilitating his plans and strategies against people and the kingdoms of God. He incessantly seeks legal right, into a person's life, by infiltrating his mind and seducing him with lies and ungodlyreasoning and by creating illusions of defeat, rejection, failure, doubt, disbelief, sickness, strife, etc. .."But of the fruit of the tree which is in the midst of the garden, God hath said, Ye shall not eat of it, neither shall ye touch it, lest ye die. And the serpent said unto the woman, Ye shall not surely die: For God doth know that in the day ye eat thereof, then your eyes shall be opened, and ye shall be as gods, knowing good and evil (Genesis 3:3-5).

When the reasoning and illusions are entertained, a door, to the soul, is opened and doubt, disobedience, fear, etc. legally enter and is conceived. These things then take root within the mind and spirit of a person and grow. This growth produces patterns of thinking and behavior that, ultimately, result in situations, circumstances, occurrences and events, as well as, the establishment of systems within a person's life, community, society and world as a whole. This is the essence of ungodly thoughts, which are not put under the subjection of Jesus Christ and the essence of idle and ungodly words that are spoken out of the mouths of people.

Divine angels come and go on command from God. God commands them to listen to and obey or not to listen to and not obey a Christian's command. The extent of their listening to and obeying a Christian is made known, to them, through a covering or mantle. A mantle identifies one's ranking and authority in the supernatural and is placed upon an individual, by the Holy Spirit, either directly or through five-fold impartations.

Words that are spoken, into the atmosphere, from an anointed servant and ambassador of God, initiates divine activity, insupport of a godly Christian lifestyle and the mandates and as-signments, given to him, by God and divine activity in op-posi-tion to diabolical warfare opposing the facilitation of his life-style and their mandates and assignments.

When entering a place, whether to minister, to work, at a social or business gathering, in prayer and even during worship, whatever the case, you must be able to discern the atmosphere of the supernatural and execute war in the realms of the spirit when necessary. You must be able to make the atmosphere conducive to your presence and assignment at any given time. You must know your weapons of warfare and when and how to operate them. You must know when and how to root out and to pull down, to destroy and to throw down, to build and to plant. (Jeremiah 1:10). You must know who is at your defense and in support of your mission and who is not, at any given time. You must know the realms that you move and operate in and the dimensions, of authority, that you have been elevated to, within those realms. You must know who and whose you are and where He wants to take you. You must be able to identify with yourself, who you are and where you are going. You must know the war you are in and be assured, that you will win, no matter how you got in or how you think you will get out. You must be convinced that "...greater is He that is in you, that he that is in the world." (1 John 4:4). You must be Christ-centered, Christ-minded and kingdom focused.

SPIRIT OF GOD

"The earth was without form, and void; and darkness was on the face of the deep. And the Spirit
of God was hovering over the face of the waters.
Then God said, Let there be. . . ."

Genesis 1:2-3a

The Spirit of God is the communicative essence of God. He
is God. He has all the characteristics of God. He is omnipresent,
omniscience and all-powerful. He can divide or extend Himself
to be everywhere at all times. He can do any number of things at
any given time. He is God in action. He can be the north wind
bringing quails and the east wind bringing plagues, all at the
same time. He can be the west wind restoring the cartilage into a
dry backsliding bone or breathing life into a lost dead soul.

The Spirit of God is God teaching, God leading, God making intercession, God empowering, God anointing, God chas-
tising, God talking, God communicating, God speaking, God
commanding and God doing. He is the windpipe of God. He is
the arm of God, the winds of God, the way of God, the hand of
God, the movements of God, the voice of God. He reveals the
mind of God and He carries out the thoughts of God. The Spirit
of God, the Holy Spirit, is God Himself, activating and manifest-
ing Himself to mankind and in the kingdom.

So, in order for the Spirit of God to be reigning in your life, you must be in Him and in relationship with Him, who is God. The spirit of mankind can only thrive and reign off of the nourishment, relationship, leadership and empowerment of the Spirit of God. Without Him man is nothing and can do nothing of value to himself or the kingdom in which he resides and is pre-destined to dominate.

The reigning of the Spirit of God in a person's life is predicated upon a person believing in Jesus Christ and accepting Him as their Lord and Saviour. He must, then, allow his life to be set apart for godly service through the cleansing of his heart and the sanctification and empowerment of their spirit.

DIVINE ACTIVITY

"Then he dreamed, and behold, a ladder was set up on the earth, and its top reached to heaven; and there the angels of God were ascending and descending on it."

Genesis 28:12

Divine Activity is angelic activity, in the realms of the super-natural, which represents God and aids and assists Christians, on God's command, in their daily living and in bringing opposition to the diabolical activity and movements.

Christians have been assigned angels, who move along the paths of the realms, in which they operate. Their assignment is to direct them, minister to them and protect them, in their day to day operations. These divine Angels have measured off a Christian's pre-determined territory in the realm of the super-natural. They are not only aware of the breath and length and depth and height of our territorial possessions, but they protect us from diabolical opposition, by engaging in warfare, on our behalf, when commanded to by God. In Zachariah 2:1 angels are seen measuring off territory for Israel.

The power and activity of Angels are dictated and released by God upon His command. Angels can change DNA, by God's delegated authority to man. This is how we can speak those things that are not, as though they were. Cancer will stop growing, cease and disappear. An army will dismantle, cease and dismiss. Strife can be bound and murders can be stopped. A bullet can be disallowed, etc. Angels know a Christian's mantle and obey his commands based on the ranking and authority which they see upon it.

Diabolical Activity

"For we do not wrestle against flesh and blood, but
against principalities, against powers, against the
rulers of the darkness of this age, against spiritual
host of wickedness in the heavenly places. Therefore take up the whole armour of God, that you
may be able to withstand in the evil day,
and having done all, to stand."

Ephesians 6:12

Diabolical activity is demonic activity, in the realms of the
supernatural, designed to prevent a person from accepting salvation and to oppose and hinder a Christian's maturity, authority,
advancement, dominion and relationship with God, as well as
the advancement of the kingdom of God in earth.

This activity must be denied, disallowed and rendered inef-
fective, by the exercising of divine authority, in the realms, of
the spirit.

Not only is there revelation knowledge, concerning information and application of mandates and assignments, but also
in handling diabolical movements and warfare, resulting from
demonic activity, in the supernatural.

Every Christian is placed along a trajectory or path, to move
in, within the spirit realms. As we move along these paths,
of territorial authority, we are attacked by demons. Ephesians
6:12 lets us know that, we war against principalities, powers,
the rulers of the darkness of this age and against the spiritual
host of wickedness in the heavenly places. They move along

our trajectory or path, as we travel in opposition of who we are and what we do for God. Diabolical activity is for the sole and specific purpose of opposing a Christian's domination and authority in specific territory within a realm and thwarting God's purpose for him in that realm and His overall kingdom purpose and advancement. This is spiritual warfare, but Paul declares in 2 Corinthians 4:8 that "we are hard-pressed on every side, yet not crushed."

Demonic opposition or diabolical activity is energized by a Christian's disobedience to God, lack of worship and lack of dimensional growth within assigned realms. This is why we must ask, seek and knock concerning God's will concerning us. (Matthew 7:7). Knocking and seeking usually results in an increased worship relationship with God and thus revelation knowledge, that otherwise would not be revealed about the realms in which they operate.

For one to pray and impart deliverance, one will have to dominate in various realms, such as prayer, worship, discernment, healing, faith, love, compassion, sympathy, empathy etc. that are relative to deliverance.

For one to operate, in the divine realms, he must be dominate over the opposing diabolical realms. If he moves in love, he must be dominate over hate, strife, selfishness etc. to name a few. Likewise for him to have authority, in the divine realm of healing, means that he also must dominate in faith, discernment, and is dominate or operates, in dimensions within that realm, over worry, sickness, oppression, depression, suppression etc. Again, a Christian dominates, in realms, by dimensions or depths of authority based on the revelation knowledge and the release, of anointing, in the realm, by God.

The unsaved and carnal Christian operates in the kingdom of darkness. He moves in diabolical realms of authority. This authority is obtained by rejecting Jesus Christ, living in sin and relinquishing his freewill, to the enemy. Because God gives mankind freewill. A person has to permit the enemy, to use him, in dark areas. Witches and other individuals, through his free-will, intentionally, allow his spirits to be dominated by Satan. Consequently, souls are infiltrated and possessed (dominated by, under the control of) by Satan and the evil spiritual hosts of whom he reigns over. In other words, when an individual chooses not to serve and worship God, he, in essence, is serv-ing and worshipping Satan. He either loves the one and hates the other. There is no in-between, as many, would like to think. It is either God or Satan. And it certainly cannot be both, as some try, through compromise. It can only be either or. It can only be either good or evil. ("No man can serve two masters: for either he will hate the one, and love the other; or else he will hold to the one, and despise the other. Ye cannot serve God and mammon). Matthew 6:24. In essence, it is the exercise of one's freewill that is the deciding and motivating agent which allows a person, to move, in the territories of darkness (diabolical) or the territories of light (divine).

Disobedience to God releases a person into the diabolical realms. In the realm (or kingdom) of darkness, the enemy op-erates according to the authority that a person releases to him by exercising their choice or freewill and submitting to him. This submission allows the enemy to use him, as well as, to what extent.

Generally both God and Satan allows a submitted person ac-cess, to supernatural authority, through the spoken word (Death and life are in the power of the tongue:..Proverbs 18:21).

There are other dimensions of mankind's submission, of himself, to God or Satan which are not being mentioned in this book.

An individual's access to the diabolical realm is obtained through the enemy using his mind and spirit. Once the enemy has influence or control, over a person's spirit, he uses it to manifest darkness or sin. He uses the person's spirit, soul and body, to do his evil bidding, against God, who is the real target of the enemy's evil.

The use of mankind is a result of Satan's desire to dethrone and his hatred for God. His goal concerning Christians is to deter them from living an abundant life, fulfilling their purpose in God and from having eternal and everlasting life in the presence of God.

Satan can never own a person's soul. He can have access to it and use its components for evil, through man's relinquishing of his free will, to him. With this access Satan uses a person's soul or his mind, emotions, will and intellect to perpetrate and facilitate his evil acts, strategies and systems throughout earth and the kingdoms of this world.

The soul belongs to God. The loss of a person's soul refers to its living forever either eternally and everlasting, in the presence of God, or out of His presence in damnation. The eternal placement, of a person's soul, is determined by the choices he makes while in his physical body on earth. Satan can offer neither eternal nor everlasting life for himself, much less mankind. His judgment, too, will be manifested.

Satan can affect the eternal place of a man's soul by deceit, lying etc. through the doors of a person's heart, which is his mind. Once he convinces a person to give him access to one's heart, he enters and has use of it and one's spirit. This is why Christians are instructed to guard their minds. "For the weapons of our warfare are not carnal, but mighty through God to the pulling down of strongholds; Casting down imaginations, and every high thing that exalteth itself against the knowledge of God, and bringing into captivity every thought to the obedience of Christ, And having in a readiness to revenge all disobedience, when your obedience is fulfilled. (2 Corinthians 10:4-6)

Every thought that seeks to enter our hearts, through our mind, must undergo a supernatural screening process. They must be spiritually discerned unto obedience to the word of God and the personality and character of Jesus Christ. In this process, what is good and willed by God is allowed access. That which is not, is either not discerned or of the enemy and must be brought into captivity (as if capturing an enemy in war); denied, disallowed, thrown down, torn down and discarded or destroyed, all to the glory of God.

If we dwell in God's secret place then our mind is protected, from demonic infiltration because Satan cannot enter the secret place of God. "He who dwells in the secret place of the Most High, shall abide under the shadow of the Almighty. ….A thousand may fall at your side, and ten thousand at your right hand; but it shall not come near you. Only with your eyes shall you look, and see the reward of the wicked. Because you have made the Lord, who is my refuge, Even the Most High, your dwelling place. No evil shall befall you, nor shall any plague come near your dwelling; For He shall give his angels charge over you, to keep you in all your ways." (Psalms 91: 1, 7-11)

In the secret place we think like God. Our thoughts are His thoughts and His thoughts are our thoughts, because we think His thoughts. We have entered His secret place (through worship) and we are protected. The mind that was in Christ Jesus is now in us. It is off limits to Satan. It has been masterfully trained to reject that which is not of God. And the enemy knows it. This is the place where the enemy cannot enter. The secret place of God. Oh, if mankind would just find his way, to the secret place, of God.

God releases authority according to His purpose for an individual in the kingdom and Satan does so as well.

As I said before, God operates according to His foreknowledge of an individual. Satan can only operate according to an individual's current availability to him. "Now, the serpent was more subtle than any beast of the field which the Lord God had made. And he said to the woman..........." (Genesis 3:1ab).

Everyone moves in either diabolical or divine realms of authority. Satan is a spirit. His nature is therefore, to move in the realms of the supernatural. Because he is fallen, he only has authority to move in areas or territory related to darkness. He can bring opposition and war in the divine realms, but he has no authority. "And behold an hand touched me, which set me upon my knees and upon the palms of my hands. And he said unto me, Oh Daniel, a man greatly beloved, understand the words that I speak unto thee, and stand upright: for unto thee am I now sent. And when he had spoken this word unto me, I stood trembling. Then said he unto me, Fear not Daniel: for from the first day that thou didst set thine heart to understand, and to chasten thyself before thy God, thy words were heard, and I am come for thy words. But the prince of the kingdom of Persia withstood me one and twenty days: but, lo, Michael, one of the chief princes, came to help me; and I remained there with the kings of Persia...But I will shew thee that which is noted in the scripture of truth: and there is none that holdeth with me in these things, but Michael your prince. (Daniel 10:11-13, 21) His defeat has already been established by God. (1John 4:4)

In Galatians 5:22-23, the Apostle Paul lists some of the realms that Christians are given authority in, to live life abundantly, eternally and fulfill God's purpose in them in the kingdom.

Likewise in Galatians 5:19-21, the Apostle Paul lists some of the realms that the enemy seduces the carnal or fleshly part of man into, so that he can use him to manifest sin and his evil works, on earth.

Anything that is not of God is of the devil. It's our choice as to whose authority we will operate in.

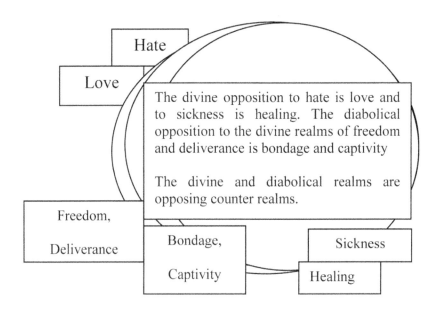

Hate

Love

The divine opposition to hate is love and to sickness is healing. The diabolical opposition to the divine realms of freedom and deliverance is bondage and captivity

The divine and diabolical realms are opposing counter realms.

Freedom, Deliverance

Bondage, Captivity

Sickness

Healing

KINGDOM AUTHORITY

> And I will give you the keys of the kingdom of
> heaven, and whatever you bind on earth will be
> bound in heaven, and whatever you loose on earth
> will be loosed in heaven.
>
> Matthew 16:19

> ...and when the man went out to the east with the
> line in his hand, he measured one-thousand cubits,
> and he brought me through the waters; the water
> came up to my ankles, again he measured...again
> he measured...again he measured...
>
> Ezekiel 47:3, 4a,5a

Kingdom authority is the authority given to mankind by God to rule over and dominate the kingdom of earth and this world. This authority is out of the kingdom of God. The ability to continuously move by the Spirit of God victoriously, accessing the resources made available, that enables one to operate in their purpose, dominate kingdoms, move in divine realms, rule over demonic realms and bring the lost to the kingdom.

It has always been the will of God for mankind to dominate in and rule over earth. With His only begotten Son, Jesus Christ as overseer, earth is an extension of the kingdom of God. In order for mankind to communicate with God, his Creator, he had to have a spirit. God is Spirit and they that worship Him, must worship Him in Spirit and in truth.

In order for mankind to rule earth, he must have access to the King's, kingdom resources, which are necessary to live abundantly, eternally and to defend the kingdom against the enemy. This access gives mankind the knowledge, wisdom, and understanding to effectively rule and communicate with the spirit world.

God, in His infinite glory, created and assigned man to rule over earth in the image of Himself, His Son Jesus Christ. Man is designed to possess the essence and the very character and personality of his creator. He is to be the epitome of the king and ruler of the Heavens and the earth. And because of that image, that likeness, he is to walk in the authority that God gave to him. This authority has been made available to him through the birth, life, death, burial, resurrection and ascension of Jesus Christ.

Walking in Kingdom authority is moving, operating, dominating, ruling, accessing revelation knowledge, exercising, activating, exerting authority, pulling down, rooting out, tearing down, destroying, throwing down, planting and building, by accessing resources, in the realms of the supernatural, based on the mantel (supernatural covering or pass that identifies one's rank and authority in any given realm of the supernatural) that God has given him. This mantle is governed by the Spirit of God and acknowledged and adhered to by the spirit world. This mantle not only signifies authority but signifies the boundaries of protection provided to the individual by God. "Now Elijah took his mantle, rolled it up, and struck the water; and it was divided this way and that, so that the two of them crossed over on dry ground." 2 Kings 2:8

To walk in kingdom authority includes the exercising of power and authority, ruler-ship, dominion, territorial domination, spiritual superiority over the realms of darkness and the ability to access the tools and resources necessary to defeat any opposition to one's mandates, assignments and overall purpose in the kingdom.

In addition, to walk in kingdom authority includes receiving the revelation knowledge needed to understand, define, interpret and release kingdom strategies, structure, dynamics, and operations.

The kingdom of earth is an extension of the kingdom of God. It has been designed to epitomize the kingdom of God. It has been designed to show forth the character and glory of God. It has been designed to look like the kingdom of God in its rulership and inhabitants.

Citizens of the kingdom are known by their likeness to the king and their adherence to his principles. "For whom He foreknew, He also predestined to be conformed to the image of His Son, . . . Romans 8:29. Kingdom citizens are appointed by the king, have assignments from the king, worship the king, adore the king, look like the king, act like the king, love like the king, dominate like the king, honor the king, pay homage to the king, understand the king, oppose what the king opposes, hate what the king hates, know the kings purpose, principles, exercise the king's power and rule over anything that offends, opposes or exalts itself against the knowledge of the king. 2   Corinthians 10:4

God's Creation, Mankind

"Then God said, "Let Us make man in Our image, according to Our likeness; let them have dominion over the fish of the sea, over the birds of the air, and over the cattle, over all the earth and over every creeping thing that creeps on the earth."

Genesis 1:26

It is God's plan for mankind to be in relation with Him, to take on His image and to walk in Kingdom authority. Man is to regain citizenry and bring the lost into their rightful place of domination and ruler-ship over the kingdom earth. God desires for man live an abundant life on earth and an eternal life in the His presence.

It has always been God's desire to be in fellowship with, His creation, mankind. From the creation, of the universe, God extended His kingship to man to make provision, for a domain, by which man would rule. No one can hold or share ruler-ship with the supreme King, the creator, God Himself. So God extended His Kingdom, the Kingdom of God, and Himself whereas He rules, in earth, by residing in mankind through the righteous acts of Jesus Christ.

Lucifer rose up against God, in a jealous rage, because he wanted to have the position that Jesus Christ had over earth and man, but in reality, Lucifer exalted himself above the Most High, God, the Father Himself. Lucifer really wanted to overtake and rule and have for His habitation, the Kingdom of God. His plan was to overtake God's throne, the angelic kingdom, the kingdom of man (heart of man) and the kingdom of earth and the worlds. In Genesis when he said , "I will exalt myself above the Most High." That is a reference to God's throne in the kingdom of God. One does not exalt himself above the most high except to be over and above the most high in position and authority. Lucifer, in essence, wanted the kingdom of God, as well as, any other subordinate kingdoms, including earth.

The Kingdom of God is the realm of authority where the throne of God is and where God resides and has seated on His right side, His only begotten Son, Jesus Christ. The Spirit of God, the Holy Spirit, God Himself occupies His kingdom's atmosphere. The Holy Spirit is the expression of God Himself. He is the expression of His presence and His glory.

Angels reside in the angelic kingdom and are allowed to move or travel to the kingdom of God for service and instructions. The angels who reside in the Kingdom of God are those who minister to and on behalf of the Godhead.

The Angelic Kingdom is the realm of the supernatural, where angels reside. Angels of light and angels of darkness are allowed to move about and roam in and throughout the region or atmosphere. The angelic kingdom is where divine and demonic angelic activity and movements originated for manifestation on earth.

Mankind is made up of body, soul and spirit. The body or outer flesh of mankind houses the soul and the spirit of man. The soul (mind, heart) of man consists of his emotions, will and intellect. The emotions, the will and the intellect of mankind are governed by what is received into the spirit of man. What is received, into the spirit of man, is based on the exercising of one's freewill and determines what comes forth from man. Thus the spirit of man reigns and releases according to what man wills him to receive from the supernatural realms.

Mankind: male and female, the human, is the spiritual and earthly creation of God. They are the kings and rulers of God's territory earth. They are the citizens of the Kingdom of God and the rulers of the kingdom of earth.

The dominion of man is exercised though communication with the Spirit of God. Each individual, walks in ruler-ship realms of authority, which have been predetermined and established by God. Man has been allocated territory and resources in the supernatural realm and this domain and ruler-ship is manifested in the kingdom of earth. Each individual must acquire his resources in the realms of the supernatural in order to complete his assignments and fulfill God's purpose in Him. Realms of the supernatural are the places, in which they may be acquired. The process is through being brought back into fellowship with God through Jesus Christ and a worship relationship with God.

It is through a worship relationship that an individual will be taught and allowed to experience and enter into the supernatural realms, necessary to acquire territory, for the kingdom. Worship will bring an individual into the presence of God. There will be an unveiling and revealing by God to the spirit of the individual who, in turn, downloads the revelation knowledge to the soul of man.

The spirit of man is taught and learns from the Spirit of God— wisdom and knowledge and application of what he has been given for manifestation. He receives outpour and overflow for manifestation, from the kingdom realm, of God, to the earthly realm for man to see, hear and experience, all to the glory of God and the manifestation and productivity of the kingdom.

It is here; it is in this place that Satan does not want to see the Christian engrossed. He launches his biggest preventive attack on mankind in the worship realm. The enemy does not want man to enter into the worship and fellowship realm with God. Satan knows that, if he does, he will be unbeatable and unconquerable. He will manifest the power and the glory of God and launch and mount up an all out war against the kingdom of darkness and win heads up. This is an attack, which Satan, the facilitator, of the kingdom of darkness, does not want to be employed or engaged in.

When man mounts up against the enemy in the way that God has ordained and predestined for him, he will be walking in kingdom authority. He will be dominating and ruling earth. He will preach the gospel of the kingdom, which is the birth, life, ministry, death, resurrection, ascension, position and authority of Jesus Christ. Satan knows that, once this is done, the war will then be over and the end will come.

The manifestation of victory will be revealed by God and the defeat of the power of darkness will be witnessed forever. This cannot take place until mankind arises and takes over in the realms that he has been predestined. This is because God in- volved him and proclaimed and spoke his inheritance when He created him. Man is a part of the plan and a part of the war therefore; he must take and do his part. God cannot nor will not change His plans regarding man's habitation of a new earth but first he must be victorious and rule in the old one.

What God spoke, in Genesis 1:26 must come to past. Man must be able to rule and handle the authority that God has given him or God will have to turn the Kingdom of earth over to the power of darkness. This is not an option for God. It will not happen. By any means necessary, God will position mankind, for kingdom domination.

To ensure mankind's domination, the Body of Christ is find-ing themselves in the midst of a paradigm shift. The shift will facilitate a transition into victory on all fronts and accounts. God, the creator, has mounted up war himself against the power of darkness and will empower mankind, His creation to fight the battle, that he has been predestined, to fight. Mankind must fight the battle, although it's the Lord's war. If man is to be a part of the kingdom of God, he must fight the part of the battle that God has assigned to him. From the Godhead to the angels to mankind, everyone and everything has a part and stake, in the war between good and evil, God and Satan.

Mankind, because of disobedience became out of fellowship with God. "For as by one man's disobedience many were made sinners, so also by one Man's obedience many will be made righteous."   Romans 5:19

The purpose of salvation was to bring mankind back into fel- lowship with God. This reinstatement enabled mankind to come into his rightful place of ruler-ship and authority so that he will fight and defeat the enemy in the supernatural realms and spend eternity in the presence of God. In the new earth and extended kingdom of God, the body of Christ must occupy their predestined territory and reign over the kingdom of earth. This extended kingdom must depict and be an epitome of the kingdom of God.

Sin has been Satan's tool for self-destruction for mankind. In it man is selfish and disobedient to God. They do not honor God in it nor do they see Him in His expressed glory. This is a tool by the enemy to keep God from His creation and to keep mankind from God.

In sin, mankind cannot operate in the spirit realm. He cannot obtain the things that God has ordained for him from the spirit realm to manifest His power and glory here on earth. Sin keeps man from his Creator. Sin blocks man's sense of what is right and what is wrong in the spirit realm.

The Body of Christ has been ordained to see from the spirit and have it manifested in the natural. But in sin, one is prone to look backwards. Man sees from the natural, therefore there is no manifestation of the spiritual. The natural cannot manifest anything for the spiritual. In other words nothing can come from or have an impact on a spiritual level based on a natural unveiling and revelation. The natural cannot produce or manifest anything in the supernatural or for the supernatural to behold.

Going backwards never works when one is aiming to go forward. We must see and experience and obtain from the supernatural realms, then it comes to past in the natural or is manifested in the natural. Sin causes man to do things backwards. This is why people cannot believe or experience all that God has for them, because it must come forth from the supernatural, before it can be realized in the natural. One must call a thing forth, from the supernatural realms, through the words of his mouth. In essence he is to call those things that are not as though they were. "....He cried with a loud voice, "Lazarus, come forth!" And he who had died came out bound hand and foot with grave clothes, and his face was wrapped with a cloth. Jesus said to them, "Loose him, and let him go." (John 11:43-44) A person must be convinced that death and life are in the power of the tongue. (Proverbs 18:21)

It has always been Satan's intention to keep the creation out of fellowship with the Creator. This will legally prevent God from extending Himself, His presence and His glory to man, His creation, because once a person is enlightened (see Hebrews 11:6), he will not go back to sin. One cannot truly partake of the supernatural realm, God's presence, His glory and revert back to a sin nature. It is impossible. There is not even a shadow of turning.

Salvation is a process that allows God to bring mankind into His kingdom realm. Through it, God teaches and allows him to experience the supernatural so that he may rule in kingdom dominion and authority. Through worship and fellowship, the individual comes into relationship with God, whereby, he is allowed to experience the supernatural things of God that will take him into extended realms and dimensions—allowing him to conquer the enemy in his realm of authority or territory as related to his kingdom purpose in God.

Citizens of the kingdom will be saved from the penalty of sin, which is separation from God forever. They will instead be a part of the ruling authority of God here on earth.

They will be saved from the presence of sin because sin has been defeated through their obedience to God and their ability, through God, to rise up and defeat the enemy. And lastly, they will be saved from the power of sin. Sin will no longer have authority over you because you walk in complete domination over it. In other words sin really has no power over us except that which we give it.

It was and remains Satan's intention to replace God. In Isaiah 14:12-14, the Prophet Isaiah depicts him this way, "How you are fallen from heaven, O Lucifer, son of the morning! How you are cut down to the ground, you who weakened the nations! For you have said in your heart: I will ascend into heaven, I will exalt my throne above the stars of God; I will also sit on the mount of the congregation, On the farthest sides of the north; I will ascend above the heights of the clouds, I will be like the Most High."

Lucifer could not and will never remove God from His throne. Not only did God create His throne, but where God is, is His throne. He is the scope of Himself. God is Creator; unlimited, all-powerful, omniscient, omnipresent and possesses the height and depth of knowledge, wisdom and authority.

Lucifer relentlessly attempted to remove God's throne from Him. He tried to eradicate the King of the Universes' citizenry. If a king has no citizens, then he has no throne. His throne is where he rules from. He can only rule if he has citizens to rule over. What authenticates a king, is property and people. God created the heavens and the earth. He is His kingdom. The enemy can only give the illusion of victory through deceit, but he will never be God nor have dominion over what God does not give him dominion over.

Lucifer tried to remove God's citizens from His kingdom by way of the angels. He was able to deceive a host of the angelic kingdom. How much easier would it be to deceive man? This is why God is so mindful of us. In addition to His unending love, God knows the force that mankind is up against and being deceived by.

With the rebellion of Satan and other angels, it became necessary for mankind to have power over darkness as well as dominate earth. For this reason, God sent Jesus Christ to bring us back into relationship with Him and give us the authority and power over the kingdom of darkness. Because Satan deceived Adam in the garden mankind lost not only his relationship with God but in losing His relationship he lost the power associated that went with being in relationship with God. If you are not in relationship with God then you are not empowered to dominate nor do you have access to revelation knowledge and grace necessary to access what you need in the spirit realm to rule over earth. So because of our fallen state we had no positive future on earth or eternally in the presence of God in the new earth.

Through the meritorious acts of Jesus Christ, we were brought back into relationship with God and assumed our rightful position as rulers of earth.

To confess Jesus Christ, is to agree and extend the will to want to come into fellowship or partnership with Him to rule over earth to acknowledge and proclaim that there are re- sources in Christ Jesus that must be obtained for this ruler-ship to take place and that you have every intention to go and get these resources so that you may walk and reign and live in the authority and abundance that God has ordained and created for His citizens.

Before you were in your mother's womb God spoke to you, about you and of you to Himself. He predestined and set in place your ruler-ship and areas of kingdom authority in reference to the overall plan that has been set forth by Him.

By confessing Jesus Christ you openly agree to and acknowledge His Sonship to God and ruler-ship over you as Lord and King. Jesus Christ is the only begotten Son of God. He is the only part of God that was taken from God and manifested in the form of a Son in equal ruler-ship and authority with Him. He thought it not robbery to be equal with God. The Holy Spirit is God from Himself. The Holy Spirit is all and every part of God that you will ever know or see while on earth.

To experience more of God, you will have to go where God is. You will have to go into the supernatural realm of God where God reveals Himself to you in mysteries and signs and wonders. This is a realm that everyone is not allowed to go, because it depends on one's relationship with God. God Himself comes to you in the manifestation of His Spirit and reveals Himself to you. You cannot receive or handle it any other way except through the spirit realm of God Himself. Any other way is a lie and the work of the enemy.

God brings Himself to you through His presence and His manifested glory. As with Moses, God brought Himself to him because he could not go to Him. The spirit of mankind was out of fellowship and relationship with God. We did not have access to the spirit realm. Now, because of Jesus Christ, we can go to God and God can come to us. Our spirit can connect to His Spirit. We have been brought back into relationship with the Godhead, because of the meritorious acts of Jesus Christ. This is why Jesus is our Lord. He owns us. He sacrificed His life for us and now we belong to Him.

How Do We Treat the Sinner?

"This is a faithful saying and worthy of all acceptance, that Christ Jesus came into the world to save sinners, of whom I am Chief."

I Timothy 1:15

When we teach and approach people for salvation we must not see and treat them as sinners, but as citizens, of God's kingdom, who must be brought into His domination and authority. If we help bring them into right relationship with God, their lives will shed the outer skin, which has been formed by the enemy, as a camouflage to their authority and rightful inheritance. If you bring them into relationship with God, the sin problem will be eradicated. They will shed the old man as snakes shed their skin. They will become new because the presence of God will purify their inner being and every part of them will come into submission to God. We have to love them and teach them and show them God and God will do the rest. He will deal with their sin. We will teach them the character and characteristics of sin without condemning them to sin. God never told us to condemn but to love.

How do we treat a sinner, do we condemn or do we love. We are to denounce and condemn sin, but the sinner we are to turn over to God, the Father and allow Him to wash and cleanse them and empower them to come into His purpose in them.

How does one seek or go after the sinner? Do we approach him with love or do we hunt him down like a barbarian? Do we condemn him and lose him or do we love him and let God use him. We must nourish him, empower him and send him forth to walk in kingdom authority and bring other citizens, to the kingdom of god to fulfill God's purpose in them.

THE POWER OF WORSHIP

"He who dwells in the secret place of the most
high, shall abide under the shadow of the almighty.
                                                    Psalms 91:1

"Oh come, let us worship and bow down; Let us
kneel before the Lord our Maker. For He is our
God, and we are the people of His pasture, and
the sheep of His hand. Today, if you will hear His
voice: Do not harden your hearts, as in the rebellion, as in the day of trial in the wilderness,
                                                    Psalms 95:6-8

Worship is the process by which a person expresses adoration, honor, admiration, accolades and gratitude to a person or
being who one believes to be of superior quality and character
to that of oneself. Worship to God is one sided and based solely,
on Him, because of who He is.

The most integral part of our relationship with God is
worship. His being and fullness are birthed in Christians
through worship. Worship positions them, for ruler-ship, in
the authoritative realms of the supernatural, which God has
ordained for them to operate, rule and have dominion. It is
impossible for Christians, to move and operate, in the realms
of the super-natural, unless they are in an intimate, worship
relationship, with God.

Worship brings a person into dimensions and depths and places in God that he never would have imagined and could never imagine going without. One cannot come to know God and the fullness of His will concerning him nor His expressed image, except through worship. It is absolutely essential, to a person's relationship, God.

The Body of Christ must see and embrace the paradigm shift that God is creating within it.

God is sending forth His prophets to teach, interpret and speak forth His word and to activate and impart gifting and anointing that will empower people to walk in kingdom authority. The Body of Christ must see themselves as spirit beings housed in a body. They must develop and maintain an intimate relationship, with God, whereas they can consistently receive revelation knowledge, concerning walking in kingdom authority, in the spirit realm and the kingdom of earth.

The Body of Christ must come to know God intimately. They must see Him. They must hear Him and they must touch Him. Christians cannot get to these places, in God, unless worship becomes an intricate part of their life. It must be a lifestyle for them. It must become as familiar and consistent to them as inhaling and exhaling. It must not be a habit, but a way of life.

As a worship lifestyle is developed, in a Christian, he will be entering into realms and dimensions of worship. The more submissive a person is to God, the more knowledgeable a person becomes of the mind and being of Him. This is coming into the presence of God. Here one will enter the presence of God. He will be like Moses in Exodus 33:18. He will experience the presence of God. God's face will be to him. He will not see God with a natural eye, but he will see Him with a spiritual eye. He will see God in the Spirit.

When in the presence of God, there is an unexplainable closeness, whereas one will know that God is there and you are in fellowship with Him. It will be as though you are in one on one conversation with Him. You will be in fellowship with the Spirit of God, which is God, Himself.

The Spirit of God is the communicative part of God. He is the created part of God that enables God to speak and communicate with other beings. The Spirit of God is His windpipe. He is to God what our windpipe is to us.

In the presence of god you are actually in communication with God. It is not a facade. It is not a dream or a vision. You are in fellowship with God. This is where you come to know God. This is where you will come into the knowledge of the depths of His personality. This is where God reveals Himself to you in ways that you otherwise would not have known. There are dimensions in the realms of worship where revelation in worship it is revelation about the person of God and His purpose and desires for you and those things which are relative to your relationship with God, others and your purpose. Revelation knowledge is available in every realm. It is available in dimensions and is accessible, to the individual, who has been given access to that realm of authority and in the predestined measure according to his purpose and assignments, within the realm, concerning the kingdom. The deeper the dimension the deeper the relationship and communication is.

Within the dimensions of the realm of worship is the secret place of God. This is a depth within the Holy of Holies. This is God's intimate place. This is a dwelling place where God gives revelation knowledge, by revealing Himself to Christians. Christians will not know that they are there until they actually find themselves in the midst of it. Christians will begin hearing revela-tion; begin hearing His voice in their ear and within the crevices of their being. It's not me, they'll say to themselves. I know it's not me. It's an inner voice. It's God. It's a knowing. It's a peace. You cannot explain it, you just want more and you know you can't do without it. You must go deeper or you'll feel as though you're in a wilderness. You must have an avenue for release. If you don't get more, you will be as a deer panting by the water brook (see Psalms 42:1). You will come into an intimate relationship with God through worship and interpret His will. God in His infinite glory has prepared a place for us to rule and dominate in under His leadership. Earth is an extension of the kingdom of God. Mankind is predestined to rule and dominate over diabolical principalities and powers.

Why We Worship

- brings us into obedience to God
- commanded to
- pleases God
- experience God's presence, His glory
- clarifies calling
- brings us into intimacy with God
- provides us release
- satisfies need to be intimate with God

Power of Worship

- develop an ear for the voice of God
- experience the presence/glory of God upon life and being
- see the manifestation of God's presence
- come to know intimately, the character, voice and movements of God
- empowered and anointed by Spirit of God
- receive revelation knowledge
- takes you into unimaginable realms and dimension of the supernatural
- spiritual perfection (maturity)

Attitude for Worship

- sacrifice
- honor
- privilege
- desire

Process of Worship

- **choose location** - should be private, time sensitive (depending on worship type)

- **create atmosphere** - praise directed at and to God only

- **prepare vessel** - prayer of repentance and submission

- **yield vessel** - address or pray to God, offering total self in worship. Also includes notifying and speaking into diabolical realms of your intentions to God and their being prohibited from taking part in any way (warfare praise is continuous as this may be a place where you may reach levels of opposition depending upon where you are in Christ). Very important to note: your personal agenda stops here as well. Worship is about God and His personal desires, as well as, His agenda for you. It is continuous adoration, to God only, in reference to Him and His mighty works.

- **submission** - totally, in all areas of your life. This is a very serious stage as you are giving God permission to reign in and over every area of your life both now and forevermore. ***This present act cannot be revoked.*** Because He is perfect in integrity, God will hold you to what you speak to Him at any given time. What God does with you in this setting is done in the spirit realm. You will see results and changes of your worship experiences on an ongoing basis throughout you life. Even if a person forgets the encounter, God doesn't. He remembers and is honest and faithful.

- **wait** - there may or may not be a lengthy visitation, or even one at all, it depends on God's agenda, your intentions for worship, your location and your availability of time. God is sensitive to your availability, which many times may not be in your control.

- **endurance** - early stages of worship may seem very tedious, but your flesh must be trained and tamed and your spirit must be trained and developed by God as well. The deeper the relationship with God the easier it is to go through the stages of preparing, yielding, submitting, waiting and enduring. After awhile it will become a lifestyle and feel as natural as breathing. In addition, no matter how close you are to God, waiting and enduring is always predicated on God's agenda when He manifests His presence. God's agenda may or may not include you. Sometimes, He may just want to be worshipped by you, or in fellowship with you, His creation.

- **lifestyle** - worship becomes such a lifestyle for you that you can do it anywhere, without notice or prompting by anyone other than the Holy Spirit, and it takes you so little time to come into fellowship with God. At the name of Jesus or the sound of worship or worship music you are like the ever-ready battery, already charged and ready to go. When you move, in this realm of worship, it feels as though God's presence upon you comes almost automatically. Often, when in corporate worship, you will find yourself having to control your inner desire to worship because the service, for various reasons, is not moving in the same realm of worship with you. This is a realm whereas a person cannot come out of worship immediately. So, if you go into His presence, you will find yourself still in a worship mode while the service has moved on. God said call me and I will answer. So you are in a place in God, when you move in worship, it is a call to God for His fellowship. He answers with His presence. It's like an Adam relationship. You are allowed to walk in the cool of the day with the Father. It is a privilege and an honor, afforded to you, based on your continuous desire and obedience for and to Him. It is a level of maturity, which must be handled in the mature manner, that God has mentored you in, through His revelation knowledge.

PRESENCE OF GOD

"Therefore I was left alone when I saw this great vision, and no strength remained in me; for my vigor was turned to frailty in me, and I retained no strength. Yet I heard the sound of his words;......"

Daniel 10:8,9a

The Spirit of God resting and/or moving upon an individual/s during predetermined times, whereas the Spirit brings a person/s from one point and takes them to another point or place in Him, for a specific amount of time, relative to His will, agenda and purpose concerning the individual/s.

"Then Moses went up into the mountain, and a cloud covered the mountain. Now the glory of the Lord rested on Mount Sinai, and the cloud covered it six days. And on the seventh day, He called to Moses out of the midst of the cloud. The sight of the glory of the Lord was like a consuming fire on the top of the mountain in the eyes of the children of Israel. So Moses went into the midst of the cloud and went up into the mountain. And Moses was on the mountain forty days and forty nights.   Exodus 24:15-18

In the Presence of God

- **be silent** – this is not the time to pray or praise. You may continue in worship for a period, but even worship will cease when your spirit is directed to do so. This is definitely not the time to talk or even think. Your flesh and diabolical warfare should have been dealt with in the worship stage of submission. However the flesh is prone to wonder and it is the nature of demons to infiltrate. Ignore them, they are low level and will have no effect in this realm unless you take your mind off the object of your worship which is God. (Peter on water). Once the presence if God is manifested, depending on your development, there is no interference or infiltration from the diabolical spirit realm (flesh cannot dwell (stay) in the presence of God.)

- **be still** – In His presence, there must not be any movement of body (except in corporate ministry, and even then very limited, if any), soul or spirit. Every part of you, your very being must be still before God and at attention, waiting for the movement of the Holy Spirit. Even the spirit of man must wait. This is the highest level of prayer and worship, total submission in God's presence.

This silent obedience is the level Jesus was at in the Garden of Gethsemane in Matthew 26:39 and Isaiah was, in the temple, in Isaiah Chapter 6.

Between me…and **not** in Matthew 26:39, **nevertheless** erupted from His silent obedience to the will and agenda of God. This is the echo the growth realm of waiting and being consumed by the presence of God. This is the highest form of submission. In the presence of God, you are totally consumed by His being, His will and His agenda. Nothing else matters, and you think of nothing else. Not your life, your loved ones, your past, your present or even your future, only God. Your thoughts will be of what God wants from you and whatever it is, even if you can't give it to Him right away. Your thoughts will be that, He can have it. I'll do it when I can. Your spirit will utter, change me, mold me, melt me and make me. I am in the potter's house, on the potter's wheel and in the potter's hands.

Note: God's agenda may cause you to continue in worship. He will speak, empower, filter, fill and empty you. He will just all out change you. You will not know endurance. (waiting for the Spirit to wit) or feel all, if any, of these things happening to you. Remember, your spirit receives from God and makes it known to your soul in time.

- **be God's** – Simply and seriously put. You belong to the potter. Please, you'll implore God, keep me on the wheel, and make me in your image. You are so submitted, at this point, that you are somewhat like Daniel in chapter 10 of the book of Daniel.

The presence of God produces an overwhelming heaviness or weight upon a person's being and manifests Himself as a consuming fire and puts in order anybody or anything that does not line up or come into agreement to His will at any given time. Even if you were not yielded, you would be at this point. No flesh can dwell in His presence, so anything in His path that is not like Him will be consumed.

Many have expressed the experience or how they feel when the presence of the Spirit of God is upon them. Although some will be similar and different, all will agree, that it is an arresting and overwhelming expression that implodes from within a person's very being. You will find that no one will have to tell you that God is real because you have surely experienced Him for yourself.

It is most often during this crucial time, before God, that many people are built-up, developed, matured, healed and delivered and empowered, as well as, receive chastisement. There will be impartations, instructions, guidance, directions, revelation knowledge, information, knowledge of God's will, and experience the essence of God's being, His glory.

God determines the length of His presence, the agenda during His presence and the participants or partakers to His presence and what He releases when he comes. Whatever takes place, it is relative to kingdom building and kingdom living.

VOICE OF GOD

"and after the earthquake a fire, but the Lord was not in the fire; and after the fire a still small voice. So it was, when Elijah heard it, that He wrapped his face in his mantle and went out and stood in the entrance of the cave. Suddenly a voice came to him, and said, "What are you doing here, Elijah?"
1 Kings 19:12-13

The voice of God radiates throughout your spirit being, while at the same time it is still, quiet, peaceful, comforting, relaxing, assuring, forceful, authoritative, no nonsense, serious. Its presence is often felt in your stomach, chest area, head and ears. People react to His voice differently but respectfully. You just know that it's not your inner voice, but His voice inside of and pressing upon you.

The more time you spend in fellowship with God, the clearer His voice will become to you. The more tuned your spirit will be to His Spirit. This is the ear to hear. A realm in the spirit, that your spirit can hear God's voice clearly, with very little or no influence, infiltration and interference from the flesh. When your spirit hears God clearly, it can receive information or revelation (see section on Revelation Knowledge) from the Spirit of God, interpret it and download it to your soul so that you can apply it, to your life and ministry, according to God's will, purpose and intentions.

Interferences to the voice of God, namely, sin, self and Satan, must be dealt with if you are to have a healthy and productive relationship with God. They must be silenced and put under submission immediately to avoid any impact from them. Paul tells us in 1 Corinthians 10:5 that we are to, "cast down arguments and every high thing that exalts itself against the knowledge of God, bringing every thought into captivity to the obedience of Christ."

GLORY OF GOD

""And he said, "Please, show me Your glory." Then He said, "I will make all My goodness pass before you,…."

Exodus 33: 18-19a

The glory of God is the expressed image, fullness and being of God. It is every part of Him. It is the essence of God producing a weight upon the essence of your very being. The glory of God is God. It is God arrayed in His being, in the essence of Himself. It is who He is. The glory of God is His every attribute and His every characteristic. It is His goodness. It is His love, joy, temperance, faithfulness, goodness, wisdom, knowledge. The glory of God is who we are to be an expressed image. This image is what we have been ordained to be conformed to.

In the glory stage of a person's relationship with God, one will not only know His voice, but will have come to know Him intricately and intimately.

The glory of God is the very essence of the creator. A Christian may know how He feels about something at any given time in any given situation. He will be so close to God that he is always aware of and discerning how and what He feels. He will be able to feel and differentiate between God's feelings and those of His own. A Christian may know how He will move or act at any given time because God is prone to share these feelings and things with him. He will share Himself with you as you fellowship and come into His presence. You will understand the stillness in His voice when He speaks to you, the quietness of His tone and the seriousness of His actions. You will feel out of sorts when you are not in His presence, while at the same time knowing that your mortality cannot endure being in His presence all the time. Life on earth will no longer be your priority, but you will find yourself longing to be with Him at any cost. You'll always want to be closer to Him, at the same time knowing that your earthly body will only let you get but so close. So instead, you just seek to fulfill His purpose in you because fulfilling His purpose in you and pleasing Him, is the next best thing to being in eternity with Him.

Not only do you long for God, but you have become aware that God longs for fellowship with you as well. So, you'll begin to understand and get use to Him coming to you-- in His presence just have you in his presence of fellowship.

Your biggest fear in life will become as David feared, in Psalm 51, Lord, don't take your Holy Spirit from me. In other words, Lord, don't take your presence from me. You will know that the worst thing that could happen, in your life, is to be out of fellowship with your Creator, God.

REVELATION KNOWLEDGE

"But I make known to you, brethren, that the gospel which was preached by me is not according to man. For I neither received it from man, nor was I taught it, but it came through the revelation of Jesus Christ."

Galatians 1:11-12

Revelation knowledge is the unveiling of supernatural knowledge, by God, to an individual with the specific intent to make Himself known to the person. It is unveiling of the mind, a person reasoning, knowledge, discernment and intentions of God and is given to release access to a Christian, to the kingdom resources, necessary for him to live an abundant life and fulfill God's purpose for him.

"Jesus answered and said to him, "Blessed are you, Simon Bar-Jonah, for flesh and blood has not revealed this to you, but My Father who is in heaven."   Matthew 16:17

To aid and insure that mankind has the tools necessary, God has made provision for them to access what they need, in the spirit realm; to walk in kingdom authority and rule accordingly as ordained by Him. The spirit of mankind has been given, to him, to enable him to fellowship with God and to re-ceive the knowledge, wisdom and understanding in reference to this kingdom that He has assigned us to. The spirit of man, allows us to communicate with God. The Holy Spirit downloads or sends information to our spirit and our spirit interprets and transmits it to us. In addition to information, there is an unveiling by God about Himself, and His kingdoms for the purpose of aiding us in kingdom ruling and accessing resources needed to rule His kingdom earth. This unveiling is called revelation knowledge. It is knowledge revealed by God to us that we would have otherwise not known. This revelation knowledge is necessary for us to move about and operate in the realms that he has assigned us to.

So many Christians are not ready to receive all that God has, to offer them, because they have not developed an intimate enough relationship with God, which is required for them to hear and receive from Him.

My people perish for the lack of knowledge. This is knowledge that comes from the Spirit of God to the spirit of man. This revelation knowledge is downloaded and transmitted, to the soul of man, for application to kingdom building and kingdom living.

Body of Christ, there is a place in God and in His kingdom where He wants us to be and that place is in the realms of the supernatural. There, they can have access to and come to know the God and source of their creation. They will come to know that it is a real place, in which mankind is to be a part of and move and operate in. They will come to know that the war between good and evil, between God and Satan is real, and God's victory in it is eminent. Moreover, they will come to know that the supernatural is real and even more so, GOD IS.

SPIRITUAL WARFARE

"For we do not wrestle against flesh and blood, but
against principalities, against powers, against the
rulers of the darkness of this age, against spiritual
hosts of wickedness in the heavenly places."

Ephesians 6:12

Spiritual warfare is the act of engaging against diabolical
satanic adversities and activities and taking authority over the
atmospheric movements caused by Satan and other diabolical
hosts and agents in the realm of the supernatural and for the
specific purpose of being manifested in earth.

God has positioned the Body of Christ to be victorious in
every area of warfare that they may encounter at any given time.
We have the word of God, the power of God, the anointing of
God and the authority of God. Each member of the Body of
Christ has been given a mantle that dictates and describes their
position in the various realms of the supernatural. A mantle is a
supernatural covering in the realm of the spirit which enables or
is the pass card for Christians to go into realms and pull down
re-sources that are needed to complete their assignments and
God's purpose in their lives.

No Christian should be surprised or afraid of movement in
the supernatural realms. Operating in and discerning supernatural activity, whether divine or diabolical should be the nor-
mal position and operation of a child of God. Why should the

Body of Christ remain clueless and powerless, while the enemy runs rampant with strategies and tools designed and more often than not, succeeding to destroy people's lives and stunting their growth and productivity in the kingdom?

A person cannot victoriously exist unless he can effectively war in the supernatural realms. God has given us the weapons and the authority. So why don't so many Christians know that?

The bible is the only perfect and thorough witness and source to engaging in spiritual warfare. I contend that spiritual warfare should be an introductory class for the new disciple. In reality, it is spiritual warfare that ushers a person into bondage in the first place.

The reason why so many Christians are being defeated daily in the same battle is because they have not adorned themselves with the warfare made available to them by the word of God. Paul admonishes the Body of Christ to put on the whole armor of God. Paul uses his military experience to convey his charge to us, but in reality, the armor in which he is talking about is of a supernatural nature which is recognized by the inhabitants of the supernatural realm.

God desires, commands and expects His body, the Church, to be in relationship Him, so that they may move in the realms and dimensions that He wills and has predestined for them.

Until then, many will remain lost and many will not experience the abundance of life that God has prepared for those who believe and openly confess, according to Romans 10:9, that Jesus Christ is His only begotten Son and that He raised Him from the dead."

ACTIVITY ASSIGNMENTS TO GROW BY

1. Make Time for God

Note: This exercise, will only work, if you will truly examine yourself and are willing to make a change, in your worship relationship, with God.

Write a schedule listing your hourly activities for the past seven (7) days.

Rate each activity:
- place a R by each recurring activity

- place a N by each non-recurring activity

- place a number 1,2,3..... by each recurring activity in order of priority

- place a number 1,2,3..... by each non-recurring activity in order of priority

- place a P by comparing each recurring and non-recurring 1,2,3,4 & 5 etc.

- Place a C by each activity that you can easily exchange for time in fellowship with God.

- Place an S by each activity that you can exchange for time in fellowship with God, that would definitely be a sacrifice.

- Place the current date by the activities that you placed a C and an S by.

Make a covenant prayer before the Lord to diligently try to replace your C and S activities with worship.

Make seven copies of this schedule. Place a copy:
1. on your bedroom dresser mirror
2. on your bathroom mirror
3. directly over, on or next to your television(s)
4. on your refrigerator
5. on the exit side of your front door
6. on your desk at work
7. in your bible as a book marker
8. Repeat this exercise in 30 days listing worship/fellowship with God on your schedule as one of your activities whether you performed it or not.
9. List three pros and three cons of striving to keep your covenant with God.
10. Prayerfully discuss with God your challenges and experiences and the advantages in your ability to keep the covenant you made with Him.

Comments:

_____

_____

_____

_____

_____

_____

2. Challenge Questions to Think About

- Is worship unto God a sacrifice, a privilege or both?

  _____

- Do you view worship as a sacrifice or a privilege?

  _____

- Do you find it easy to pray?

  _____

- Are you comfortable with God when you pray?

  _____

- Do you recognize God's voice?

  _____

- Do you view prayer as a tool to get things from God?

  _____

- Do you think worship is necessary if you pray every day?

  _____

- Can you differentiate between worship and prayer?

  _____

3. Life Application

Using the key words, as you move throughout the day, place yourself in these movements. Listen for the voice of God as He speaks to you.

Comments   Day 1

_____

_____

Comments   Day 2

_____

_____

Comments   Day 3

_____

_____

Comments   Day 4

_____

_____

Comments   Day 5

_____

_____

Comments   Day 6

_____

_____

Comments   Day 7

_____

_____

1. Did you hear God speak to you from this lesson? If yes, specify area/s _____. This is an indication of where God's agenda is concerning you at this time.

2. Write 3 insights that you received from this lesson.

1. _____
   _____
   _____

2. _____
   _____
   _____

3. _____
   _____
   _____

3. List 3 things that you plan to change and/or enhance as a result of this lesson.

1. _____
   _____
   _____

2. _____
   _____
   _____

3. _____
   _____
   _____

Congratulations, you are on your way, to moving in REALMS AND DIMENSIONS OF THE SUPERNATURAL, with God. Establishing a consistent worship lifestyle is essential to walking in kingdom authority. I pray God's continuous blessings upon, as you maximize, living life abundantly and walking in the Kingdom authority that He has ordained for you.

My earnest prayer is that the people of God will seek the glory of God and will come to know Him and the power of His resurrection. I pray that they will walk in the kingdom authority and domination that has been entrusted to them. I pray that they will fulfill God's purpose in them.

I further pray that every reader of this book will finish it with a more clear understanding and commitment to finding a deeper place in God and the realms of the supernatural. I pray that each will emerge declaring and proclaiming, a concerted effort and an intense commitment to come into the knowledge, of the realms and dimensions of the supernatural, which God has ordained for their life.

In Jesus Christ's Name,
Amen

To order additional copies of

Realms and Dimensions of the Supernatural
or for Book signings and Speaking engagements

Janice Fountaine Ministries
(240) 965-7810

or e-mail
fountainej@aol.com

or order online at
www.janicefountaineministries.com

Cover photography and design by:
Fred Dillard
youriphoto@yahoo.com

CPSIA information can be obtained
at www.ICGtesting.com
Printed in the USA
LVHW04s2323250918
591365LV00008B/164/P

9 781589 302426